Sleepless Nights in the Depth of the HELLSCAPE

Kate Taylor Dickinson

BOOKLOVER
PUBLISHING HOUSE

Sleepless nights in the depth

of the hellscape.

A poetry collective wrangled

together by

Kate Taylor Dickinson

Forward :

Mental illness and sin can go hand in hand. Symptoms can be confusing to the uneducated. That is what this book is about. How trauma shapes emotional transactions in strange and confounding ways.

This book isn't about darkness, the dark is far too romantic. This is about the platonic bond bringing together two people.

How relationships start off by two strangers glancing at each other. Seeing the way the other interacts with the world and coming to an understanding in a nonphysical way that you both are in need of the other.

This book is about a journey of guiding someone through their own sins as represented through the nine levels of Hell. Not as traditional sins, but as systems built through responses to trauma. Mental illness can often mirror each other with slight differences making them hard to tell one from the other. Two people seeing each other's weakness and strengths and standing strong against the storms that cloud the other's mind.

(Pick your vice, pick a poem. Whatever sounds nice.)

TABLE OF CONTENTS.

Circle Seven. Silence doesn't mean acceptance.

It means our complaints can be ignored.

Circle Eight. Run away from the mirror, she lies.

Circle Nine. Dirty little silly games.

Back on Earth. The game was still ongoing.

Earth side. On Earth as it is in

Heaven.

I wonder how you felt the first time you were left behind. New and scary thoughts, singing gracefully through old abandoned castles. Like lullabies sang to ghost children, still holding their blankets. For you too, were but a baby. Who deserved to feel safe in their bed, but instead you got a dirty hotel and people you couldn't trust.

As you got older, people walked in and almost skipped out on you gleefully it seemed. Taking with them pieces of your self esteem.

Time took its toll on your love languages and reasons to trust your elders.

I like to think that somewhere someone was watching. They made me. They built me to be kind and caring. Loving and soft. They gave a brain to match yours. A little different but still just as confused. Then they placed me in your path.

I'm sorry it took me so long to find you. I was stuck in traffic but it'll all be ok now. I'm not going to leave you, not ever. I will hold out my hand. All you need to do is let me love you. Maybe if you listen you'll learn to expect the kind of love you really deserve.

Circle one. The Limbo.

We moved by guiding each other through our own sins like Dante guided Virgle through the nine circles. Accepting each other badges of terror like we would be able to prove my bravery. But you and I can only stand frozen in limbo for so long, before we are forced to face our sins head on. Going through our symptoms like sins.

So I watched you stuck doing the limbo, as you watched me do the same. The grand dance of will they, won't they. It seems like an adventure. A huge task built on the false hope of they will. Moving under obstacles and through hoops.

I stood by watching the carefully coordinated dance. Guiding you past the times they didn't and being carefully guided through the times that people let me down.

Together we moved past mountains. Ushering in forever, playing with each other like dolls. Moving each with power and earth shattering will. Hoping to continue being playmates under the next full moon. Calling into the night, like summoning Bloody Mary to scare away our demons, because we didn't always answer each other's prayers.

Circle two. The Dance of Demons

and the Dark.

Mermaids in some art are beautiful, long hair goddesses of the deep. Skillful swimmers, gliding through waters and building beautiful nests in coral. You were never that kind of mermaid. A siren, a slinky and skilled craftsmen of lust.

With stormy eyes, stealing sailors from their slumber. The siren you became beacons me from safety. Raging seas and choppy waves, billowing winds running, like your inability to follow through. The game was set. Your points were matched.

I clung to rocks. Daring you put them away and listen with your heart. Begging those around you to speak in hushed tones to not drown in your self hate filled waters.

Love is what's left when lust falls away. But you never swam past it, in our lives we will follow your song it seems

Circle three. The Glutton for

Punishment.

When people think of gluttony the thought of consumption immediately goes to food. Of food and fine places to visit. We both rarely ate more than the minimum, so we found other things to consume.

The way you consumed pain shook me to a deep part of my core, never ending were the ways your heart could ache.

As a chef, you built recipes for disaster out of seemingly thin air. Pulling from the places in society's underbelly with the rare kind of arrogance that came from thinking you could fix people. The same exact brand I bought from the store and saved for you, I too saw the good and thought I could become its savior.

Even though we rarely stopped long enough to fix ourselves. Giving everyone tiny lines of blissful grace.

The kind of long lines you once devoured without concern for public safety. I started to end my own abuse, so maybe I could save you too.

Circle four. Gambling ways and the

lack of foresight

While your Greed sat you down at gambling tables, leaving with less than you entered with. Mine sat me down at people's feet. For our Greed wasn't even. Mine bubbled to the surface.

Greed sat dormant inside of you.

Breathing and expanding into relationships, like breath play. Needing to be the only body. Even if only being used for it, and its parts. Only gathering in non aggressive and abnormal ways, like bees in swarm season.

My greed made it hard for me to be able to tell good attention and bad attention apart.. for any press was good press, when you wanted those around you to circle you like the sun. Wanting to be the center of their universe without having to make them the same.

For I allowed you the freedom to venture outwards. Stretching your wings into far and wide adventures only to return when you needed a soft place to rest your wings. Arms opening up and allowing you to be seen as broken, without having to worry about needing fixed.

Circle five. Anger and violence

Lead-footed rage could feel like an over extended show of power. Like a dull roar replacing your normal bell-like, chime of a voice. Full of life and passion for every once and a while even you knew you had to push past your normal nice and complicated ways, because charm could fail you.

In those moments of rage, you were a God crafting control over a situation. Finally obtaining the very thing you didn't used to have, the control you had once had taken from your fragile and small body. Babies in cribs rarely are granted the luxury of control, but some even less than others when the very adults that promised

to save them, brought them pain.

       Painted across the faces of those they

were left with.

So now all that anger was simmering like a

watched pot, and even though you watched it,

sometimes it boiled over. Just like it boiled over

in me.

       Seeing the way your rage, consumed like

wildfire made my own short lived wrath feel like

it didn't go unnoticed. Like just because it lived

for a short time. The candle in the bell jar still

burned bright.

It could leave a scar.

Circle six. Hersey came down from heretics. In them they held their own sins.

If you held strongly to the older beliefs, we would have burned at stake. The few, the proud and deeply destroyed, held on to the thought that we were the grandchildren of the witches not burned.

For in historical settings we were the very girls burned at stakes, punished for our differences. Our only difference was being given a burden of minds that didn't play nicely with everyone. All the time.

My ADHD and your personality crossing the borderline made us targets.

But we found each other favorable in our ways. My mind's need to be compassionate. Empathic gave your mind's gift of pushing away people a soft and pleasant field in which to plant your fairy rings.

But still they found us harlots in which to throw their stones. Casting their own sins out at us like padding thoughts.

Just *"grow up, grow tougher, thicker skin"* and *"maybe we will adapt better to our surroundings."* But we had been tough, had been strong. Had lost control too many times. So we controlled each other's reactions.

So we had grown, grown to never allow

someone to feel that brand of guilt for gifts that

couldn't be returned. In our lights, we feasted.

Circle seven.

Silence doesn't mean acceptance.

It means our complaints can be

ignored.

Through our existence fighting for our right to stand in the sun, it has made some people see our glimmering presence as the fire of passion, disguised as violent acts of rebellion.

Almost as though our violence exists in numbers. Has become a calling card to gain needed ground. We fight for our right, to be heard, to be taught about.

Our minds bend thoughts in circles, racing after each other like cars stuck on a track. Building bridges in the sand, but never stepping foot off the island.

You closed yourself down, seeing the world the same way it saw you. An unpredictable goddess of wrath and anger. For you were fragile in the way Bombs were.

Set and able to explode. But violence has often struck you back. In being jumped in dark alleyways or being beaten for standing up for yourself after you exploded.

Violence can also contain beauty, in wildfires that sweep the landscape and create bare and open places for new growth to occur. Maybe what I'm saying is that not all Violence is evil. Not all anger is an over reaction. Sometimes it's a symbol of being too kind for too long. A gentle reminder that most people remember your violence over repeated kindness, but they would remember.

Circle eight. Run away from the mirror, she lies.

The imposter clown comes to play. "Sit here with me and fret your life away. You were never that special anyways." He chattered away, making up stories to keep getting his way. The fraud in the mirror begged me to climb inside, the imposter clown with all of his lies .

Your imposter syndrome played nicely with mine. It made us both feel like we weren't good enough for the other. As though we weren't a set of twins seeing each other's minds as equals.

Where my Adhd and your BPD intersected we were at the crossroads of time.

Impulsive behavior, our quick witted anger, our compassion and the vast feeling of being constantly misunderstood. Our minds used like play things, where they were used as an excuse by those playing pretend. By people never looking passed the silly symptoms on to the ones that tore us to shreds.

No one claimed the anxiety that came, or depression. The overwhelming feeling of letting everyone down by slipping into a keyhole of self doubt. The high probability of people vanishing into the dust when you simply forgot they cared.

But the Imposter Clown played for keeps, tidying up memories he used to creep back inside just when things went well, to remind us of our sins and the nine circles of Hell.

How sin can just be our disorders also playing for

keeps, keeping us in chains.

What little thieves.

So we slept bundled up in the cold, still

night. Maybe tonight, I'll sleep so much better

surrounded by lights.

Circle nine. Dirty little silly games.

In all of the treacherous games that we play. Fooling each other, then running away. It wasn't a purposeful thing that we did. Laughing and shouting. Acting like kids.

For once we were allowed to act out with each other. Playing games, like we didn't have feelings to bother.

I promised not to leave, then I left for a while. I came back when I needed a smile. You played the same games, often playing them better. But you knew that I wouldn't leave you. It was like we took vows, and locked them up tight. Playing for fun and playing for keeps. Keeps vows of treachery.

Back on Earth. The game was still ongoing.

Nothing was as valuable of a creator then time. Stretching across the measures of wounds, healing open and fresh cuts made by lashing out tongues.

I told my mind to *"stop screaming, for I couldn't drown out the noise begging me to finish up quickly and make very little mess."* Torture of bouncing between thoughts. The same way you do, going between thinking the other didn't care about others' behavior because we didn't care about each other or if we didn't care because we understood.

Trying to fathom the tombstones. Our dates laid in concrete written over so many times

I failed to see the dates any longer. Almost two years spent tangling each up in the ropes of our thoughts. Hidden by noises from nearby crowds, but still you haunted me.

Our nine levels were completely written out in two days. Summing a lifetime of flaws down played by man. Down played by each other, now that I mapped out our journey. I knew now that the ending would never come. That we were too entangled. But maybe just maybe. The cycle won't continue.

Kate Taylor Dickinson :

Author bio :

When I started writing, I was in high school. Unsure of my own voice, who I was or who I wanted to become. All I knew was that I was a shy, emotional teenager who kept her distance from those around her. Then I grew up, grew into a person who kept her pop punk roots. Got several tattoos and found out what I wanted to write about. At least for now, as an adult with ADHD I am becoming more comfortable with the concept that I am not always going to know what I want. With that Kate Taylor Dickinson was born. Little by little she took on the complicated task of being my god complex, the little part of my ADHD that knew who she was at all times. The thing that wasn't afraid of failure. Too self inflated to accept anything less than success. If I was honest this person always lived inside me, for the first time I was allowing her to come to the surface.

The public face of me isn't that far off from who I really am. In a lot of ways it's as if I created her to block me from the things that I can't comprehend, like non death loss and the unbelievable amount of pain that betrayal can bring. This book serves as the bridge between hope and happiness. What could be, and what is. Life isn't always easy, but it's always worth it.

Dear little reader.

As the sleepless nights creep. Here's a book you

can keep. You can read it fast, or read it slow.

Hiding inside are some things you need to know.

Keep her close when things get rough. You, my

little street fighter, are very tough.

Love always.

Kate Taylor Dickinson